W9-ALU-798

DATE DUE

My Heart Is
Full of Wishes

Story by Joshua Grishaw
Illustrations by Lane Yerkes

RSVP

RAINTREE
STECK-VAUGHN
P U B L I S H E R S
The Steck-Vaughn Company

Austin, Texas

For my mom and dad, who always told me that I could be whatever I set my goal to be and whom I love with all my heart and soul. Also, to all the kids in the world who have to fight against illnesses but who never stop wishing. — J.G.

For my two sons, Christopher and Jonathan, with a father's love — L.Y.

Printed in Mexico.

1 2 3 4 5 6 7 8 9 0 RRD 99 98 97 96 95 94

Library of Congress Cataloging-in-Publication Data

Grishaw, Joshua, 1983-
    My heart is full of wishes / story by Joshua Grishaw; illustrations by Lane Yerkes.
      p.   cm. — (Publish-a-book)
    Summary: A young boy with cystic fibrosis describes some of his fears and his dreams for a better life.
    ISBN 0–8114–7269-8
    1. Children's writings, American.   [1. Cystic fibrosis —Fiction.   2. Wishes — Fiction.
3. Children's writings.]   I. Yerkes, Lane, ill.   II. Title.   III. Series.
PZ7.G88795My   1995
[Fic] — dc20

94-40435
CIP AC

You know the old saying, you can never judge a book by its cover. Well, sometimes I think that they must have written that saying just for me. Because when people look at me, they see a skinny little kid wearing glasses. I guess they would even say I look sort of nerdish, but that is not what I'm really like at all. Inside, my heart is full. It's so full it's like a gigantic helium balloon that's bursting with the most amazing thing. It's bursting with wishes!

You see, I'm not your average, run-of-the-mill, normal, everyday kid. I'm a kid who has to fight against an enemy that I can't see. I fight against an illness that I was unlucky enough to be born with. I battle against cystic fibrosis. It's a long, hard, uphill fight, and a lot of the time while my body is busy fighting against C.F., I have to just lie around to give my body the strength it needs. But in my mind the action never stops. The wishing mixes with my imagination and wow! What excitement there is!

One day I wished that I was a knight. I saw myself as Sir Lancelot. I was riding on a magnificent horse and I had a magic sword in my belt. A beautiful princess was about to be eaten by a fire-breathing dragon. The princess was tied up to a sacrificial post and left all alone in the wicked black forest. She was crying for help, but all the brave knights who tried to help her were unable to get by the fire-breathing dragon before they were thrown aside like rag dolls.

8

I mustered up all the courage that was way down deep in my soul and I shouted, "Begone, you evil dragon!" I stabbed the dragon in his cruel, black heart. The black forest suddenly turned into a green forest with birds singing in the sky. The beautiful princess said, "My hero! You saved me!"

In the spring when I'm playing Little League ball, I often wish that I were a great ballplayer. Our team is down 10–9, and it's up to me. The whole team is yelling my name, "Josh, JOSH, **JOSH**!" They are expecting a miracle. The parents are biting their fingernails, yelling, "You can do it!" It's my turn at bat, bases are loaded, and I have the final bat of the game.

I come up to the plate. The pitcher looks at me and grins. He's not really seeing me. He is just seeing my size. He thinks, "I can get this little skinny kid." He doesn't know that I have more guts, determination, and drive than all the players on both teams. He rears back and lets the first pitch go. I think it's low. "Strike one!" yells the umpire. The other players moan. The parents shout, "That's okay—now you see it—put your eye on it—you can do it!"

I try to calm myself. My palms are sweaty and slippery on the steel bat. The sun is so hot I think I hear my sweat sizzling on the bat like an egg frying in a hot skillet. Here comes the next pitch. It looks low, too, but I've got to try. After all, the umpire called the last one a strike. I swing and feel nothing but the empty air. "Strike two!" the umpire's menacing voice screams. The parents are now shaking their heads. The players' heads are bowed, their faces white with tears beginning to form in their eyes.

13

The players on the other team are grinning, smacking their bubble gum, and chanting, "Strike him out, Chaz! Yeah, you're the man!"

The pitcher, Chaz, leans back, full of confidence, and throws the final pitch. I hear the ball breaking through the air before it gets to the bat. I close my eyes and pray. I swing the bat — contact! The steel bat smacks against the hard ball. Zoom! The ball flies over the fence.

Laughter and cheers erupt from the parents, teammates, and coach. After I touch home plate for the grand slam home run, I am carried on the shoulders of my coach. Everyone crowds around me offering congratulations. Wow! What a wish! Or maybe this is really a dream?

I love to lie on my bed on warm summer nights and listen to the crickets chirp and the whippoorwills call out to one another. A slight breeze blows my curtain away from the window. It's dark and I'm all alone.

I can hear my dad snoring from the other bedroom. I really wish I could get up and cuddle up between him and my mom, but I'm ten years old now and I'm supposed to sleep in my own bed. Sometimes I wish that I was a little kid again so things like that would be okay. I'd like to be a big kid again when morning comes.

The night is the time I need my mom. Night is when I think I see monsters coming out of the bedroom closet. The dark makes shapes appear and take the form of different types of monsters. The monsters reach out at me, and I scramble to turn on my lamp so they will disappear. Monsters are scared of the light. The light makes the monsters disappear, but when I turn off the lights, there they are again.

I shut my eyes and I say my prayers, starting, "Now I lay me down to sleep." I always end with "God, please cure C.F." I keep my eyes squinted tight and turn to go to sleep. I have tried to reach down deep inside of myself to find courage, but it's just too dark, and I'm too alone.

Finally, I crawl out of my warm but unrestful bed and run into my mom and dad's room. I put my hand on my mom's face and whisper, "Mom, I'm scared." She does what she does every time I come into her room in the middle of the night. She reaches up and feels my forehead to see if I'm sick and have a temperature. She finds out that it is cool, and she opens up the covers and pulls me down beside her. She tells me to think nice, happy thoughts because those dark monsters don't like happy thoughts.

We talk about our summer plans of visiting the beach and I fall asleep so happy that I'm wishing, wishing, wishing that I was on a sandy beach, with the waves rolling into the sand, licking and lapping at my toes. I don't seem to notice, though, because I am too busy making my sand castle, which even has a moat around it like a real medieval castle.

Suddenly, a lifeguard comes over to me and gives me a gold medal to hang around my neck because I won the contest for the most brilliant and magnificent castle of all. The bright sun is shining down and making everything glisten. I see a pretty brown-haired girl, and she wants to help me build more castles. We laugh and throw sand at each other. Wow! What a dream! Was I wishing for a girlfriend?

When school is out and the days are long, I lie on my back in the fresh-cut grass and stare way up high in the sky and watch the pillowy white clouds roll by. I try to imagine what the cloud shapes could be. I see angels, dragons, people, and animals.

I wish I could fly up there and go to sleep on a cloud. It would feel like a great big pillow and when I would awake, I would turn over and watch all the people down on Earth scramble back and forth, looking like ants in their little ant-like cars. I would wonder what their lives were like and if they were full of wishes just like mine.

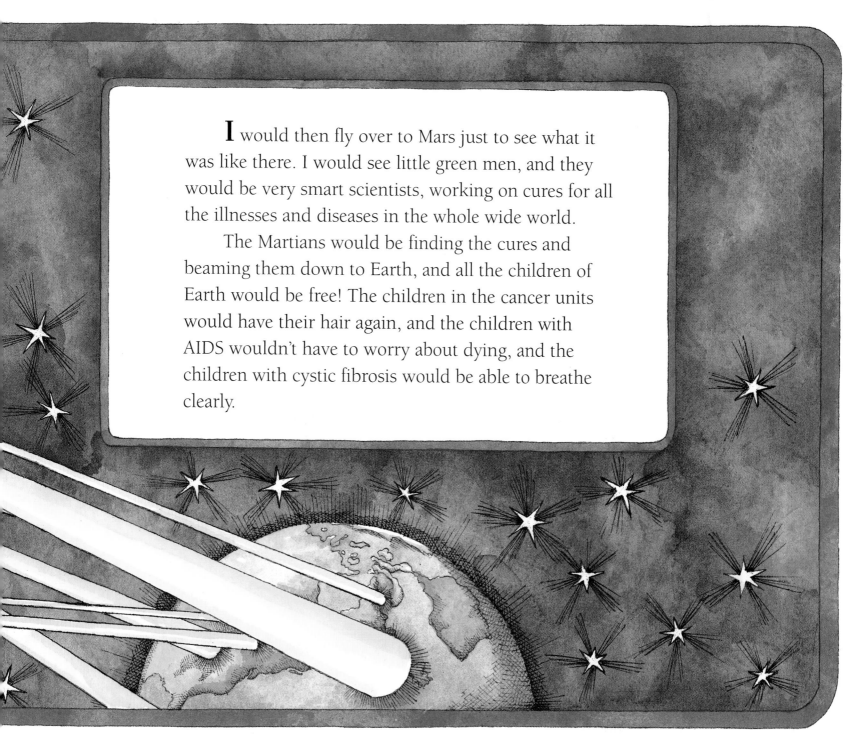

I would then fly over to Mars just to see what it was like there. I would see little green men, and they would be very smart scientists, working on cures for all the illnesses and diseases in the whole wide world.

The Martians would be finding the cures and beaming them down to Earth, and all the children of Earth would be free! The children in the cancer units would have their hair again, and the children with AIDS wouldn't have to worry about dying, and the children with cystic fibrosis would be able to breathe clearly.

We would all be free from hospitals, needles, and medicines. We would be free to be kids—to kick up our heels and run in the fields, to go swimming in the creek and fishing in ponds. It will be wonderful, and this is my greatest wish. No more tears or fears. No lying in beds while all the normal kids are outside playing. No more putting our lives on hold until we get out of the hospitals or until we feel better. No more letting these diseases win. We win. It is our victory! And we stand proud, our hands raised in triumph like the king of the mountain, our greatest wish fulfilled.

I have so many wishes. Wishes that I'll be an Eagle Scout. Wishes that I'll be married and a father of eight kids. That I'll be a grandfather. That I will help my dad run a steel business. And that I'll always have my mom and dad with me.

My heart bursts open with wishes: wishes that keep me from being afraid, wishes that carry me to far-off lands, and wishes that make me a hero. I'll just keep thinking up wishes, wishes, wishes until my heart can't hold any more.

Joshua Grishaw, author of **My Heart Is Full of Wishes**, has a very vivid imagination that sometimes gets him into big trouble, but more often helps him create remarkable stories. He has always enjoyed writing and has won awards in the "Young Authors" contest every year since kindergarten. As a fifth-grader, Joshua was sponsored in the 1994 Publish-a-Book Contest by Mrs. Suzanne Blackwell of Madison Heights Library, Madison Heights, Virginia.

Joshua finds that having cystic fibrosis is a nuisance, but he doesn't let it get in the way of being an all-American boy. He has been an active member in the Boy Scouts for the past four years and has earned 21 special badges and awards. He is an honor student who enjoys baseball-card collecting and any kind of fishing.

Joshua loves playing baseball. He was an Amherst All-Star in 1993, and in his first year in major league in 1994, he was chosen as an alternate. Even though he may be the smallest boy on the team, he lives by the motto, "Rarely is the most powerful of us the strongest."

Joshua is "pure country." He loves country music, his two cats, and his beagle, named Bruiser. He has grown up in a small rural community called Pleasant View with his parents, William and Crystal. His school has only one hundred students. His proudest moment will be when he sees his book in print.

The twenty honorable-mention winners in the **1994 Raintree/Steck-Vaughn Publish-a-Book Contest** were Dennis J. Lee, Bowen School, Newton, Massachusetts; Jessica Stephen, Harborside School, Milford, Connecticut; Cassandra Gaddo, Southview Elementary School, Waconia, Minnesota; Emily Hinson, Robert E. Lee Elementary School, East Wenatchee, Washington; Jessie Manning, Rice Lake Elementary School, Maple Grove, Minnesota; Neil Finfrock, Brimfield Elementary, Kent, Ohio; Andrew Campbell, St. Eugene's School, Santa Rosa, California; Tiffany McDermott, St. Rose of Lima School, Freehold, New Jersey; Laura Dorval, Riverside Middle School, Chattaroy, Washington; Alison Taylor, Fisher Elementary School, Oklahoma City, Oklahoma; Kendra Hennig, East Farms School, Farmington, Connecticut; Lisa Walters, Northeast Elementary School, Kearney, Nebraska; Hunter Stitik, Forest Oak Elementary School, Newark, Delaware; Jamie Pucka, Rensselaer Central Middle School, Rensselaer, Indiana; April Wagner, Monte Vista Middle School, San Jacinto, California; Elizabeth Neale, Clifton Springs Elementary School, Clifton Springs, New York; Rachel Kuehn, Roseville Public Library, Roseville, California; Carolyn Blessing, John Diemer School, Overland Park, Kansas; Kelsey Condra, Grace Academy of Dallas, Dallas, Texas; Michael Gildener-Leapman, Charles E. Smith Jewish Day School, Rockville, Maryland.

Lane Yerkes graduated from the Philadelphia College of Art in 1972 and began his career as a freelance illustrator. His assignments have covered editorial, newspaper, advertising, book publishing, fabric design, and magazine illustration. Lane is married with two sons and maintains his studio on the southwest coast of Florida, where he lives.